GUSTAV MAHLER

SYMPHONIES NOS. 3 and 4

IN FULL SCORE

DOVER PUBLICATIONS, INC., NEW YORK

Published in Canada by General Publishing Company, Ltd.,
30 Lesmill Road, Don Mills, Toronto, Ontario.
Published in the United Kingdom by Constable and Company, Ltd.

This Dover edition, first published in 1989, is a republication
of the editions published by Universal Edition, Vienna, n.d.
The poetic texts, the lists of instruments, and the footnotes in the score
have been newly translated, and a glossary of German terms has been provided.

Manufactured in the United States of America
Dover Publications, Inc.
31 East 2nd Street
Mineola, N.Y. 11501

Library of Congress Cataloging-in-Publication Data

Mahler, Gustav, 1860–1911.
[Symphonies, no. 3, D minor]
Symphonies nos. 3 and 4.

In full score.
The 1st work for alto, women's chorus, boys' choir,
and orchestra; the 2nd for soprano and orchestra.
Text of the 1st work, 4th movement: Also sprach
Zarathustra / Nietzsche, 5th movement: Es sungen
drei Engel, from Des Knaben Wunderhorn; 2nd work,
4th movement: Das himmlische Leben, from Des Knaben
Wunderhorn; also printed as texts with English translations.
Reprint (1st work). Originally published: Vienna : Universal Edition, 1906.
Reprint (2nd work). Originally published: Vienna : Universal Edition, 1906.
1. Symphonies—Scores. 2. Nietzsche, Friedrich
Wilhelm, 1844–1900—Musical settings. I. Nietzsche,
Friedrich Wilhelm, 1844–1900. II. Mahler, Gustav,
1860–1911. Symphonies, no. 4, G major. 1989.
M1001.M21 no. 3 1989   89-755121
ISBN 0-486-26166-2

Contents

Glossary

(The words appear here exactly as they appear in the score.)

ab, off
abdämpfen, damp
aber, but
abnehmend, waning
abreissen, break off, flag
alle(s), all
allmählich, gradually
als, like, than
alten, old
am, at the
an, to
andern, others
Anfang(e), beginning
Anfangstempo, opening tempo
angebunden, played at the same time
Anmerkung, note
anmuthig, gracefully
anschwellend, crescendo
anzuschlagen, to be struck
As, A♭
auf, on, for
aufgehob., aufgeh., aufg., raised
aufgestellt, placed
aus, from
(sich) ausbreitend, broadening out
Ausdruck, expression
ausdrucksvoll, expressively
ausgeführt, played
auszuhalten, to sustain
B, B♭
Bässe, double basses
bedächtig, deliberate
befestigt, attached
beginnen, begin
behaglich, comfortable
bei, on
beide, both
beinahe, almost
besonders, especially
Betonungen, accentuation
bewegt, animated, agitated
bewegter, più mosso
Bewegung, motion, tempo
bezeichneten, marked
bis zum, until the
bitterlich, bitterly
bleiben, remain, *bleibt,* remains
Bogen, bow
brechen, arpeggiate
breit, broad, broadly, *breiter,* more broadly
Celli, cellos

Cis, C♯
Consonanten, consonant
Dämpfer, mute, mutes, muting
das, the
dasselbe, the same
dem, den, the
der, the, of the, who
Des, D♭
deutlich, clearly
die, the
diesen, this
Dirigenten, conductor
dirigiren, conduct, beat
doch, but
Doppelgriff, Dopplgr., double stop
drängend, pressing, *drängender,* more pressing
dumpf, muffled, dull
durch, (obtained) through
durchaus, throughout
eben, just previously
ebenfalls, likewise
ebenso, just as
Echoton, echo tone
edlen, noble, exalted
eilen, hurry, *ohne zu .eilen,* without hurrying
eilend, hurrying
eine, einem, a, one (player)
einer, eines, of a
einige, several
(sich) entfernend, becoming distant
Entfernung, distance
Empfindung, feeling, emotion
empfunden, (deeply) felt
entschieden, resolute
erste(n), first
ersterbend, dying away
Es, E♭
etwas, somewhat
Ferne, distance
feurige, fiery
Fidel, medieval fiddle
Figuren, figures
Fis, F♯
Flag., harmonics
fliessend, flowing
folgend, following, in keeping with
fort, continuing
fortlaufend(er), running, continuous
frei, freely
freihängend, suspended
frisch, vigorous, lively
früher, earlier
für, for

furchtbarer, formidable
ganzes, full
ganzlich, completely
gebrochen, arpeggiated
gebunden, legato
gedämpft, damped
gedehnt, drawn out
gehalten(en), held, held back, meno mosso
gehaltener, more restrained
geheimnisvoll(er), mysterious
gehen, go
gemächlich, comodo, easily, *gemächlicher,* più comodo
gemässigt(e), moderate
geringste, briefest
gerissen, cut off
Ges, G♭
gesangvoll, cantabile
gesättigten, saturated
geschlagen, struck
gestimmt, tuned
gestopft, gest., stopped
gestrichen, bowed
gesungen, sung
getheilt, geth., divisi
getragen, solemn
Gewalt, power
gewirbelt, rolled
gewöhnlich(e), ordinario, normally
Gis, G♯
gleichen, equal-sized
gleichmässiger, even
grell, shrill
Gr. Fl., flute
Griffbrett, fingerboard, sul tasto
grob, coarsely, rudely
grossem, grosser, great, large
grössere, larger
gut, quite
H, B
Halbe, (beat in) half-notes
Hälfte, half (of a string section)
Halt, pause
hart, hard
Hast, haste
Haupttempo, principal tempo
Hauptzeitmass, principal tempo
herausgestossen, thrust out
hervortretend, hervortr., prominently
hier, here, *von hier an,* from here on
hinaufziehen, approaching from below
hinunterziehen, approaching from above
hoch, high

höchster, greatest

hohe, high

Höhe, elevation, *in die Höhe, i. d. Höhe,* up, in the air

höher, higher

Holzbläser, woodwinds

Holzschlägeln, wooden mallets

hörbar, audible

im, in, in the

immer, always

ja, absolutely

kaum, barely

keck, bold

keine, no

klagend, lamenting

Klang, sound

kleine, small

klingen, ring

klingt, sounds

Kopfstimme, head voice

Kraft, Kraftentfaltung, power

kräftig, robustly

kurz(er), short

Lage, position

lange, long

langhallenden, long-resounding

langsam, slow, *langsamer,* slower

(sich) lassen, allow

lebhaft, lively

leidenschaftlich, passionately

leise, softly

letzten, previous

lustig, merry, merrily

Marsch, march

mehr, more

mehrfach besetzt, several to a part

merklich, noticeably

mit, with

mittlere, medium, middle

möglich, possible

möglichst, as . . . as possible

munter, cheerfully

Musiker, musician

nach, (retune) to

nachgeben, broaden

nachhorchend, listening

nachlassen, relax

Nachschlag, Nachschl., turn (at end of trill)

nachzuahmen, to imitate

(sich) nähernd, drawing nearer

Naturlaut, sound of nature

natürlich, ordinario

nehmen, take, change to

nicht, not, don't

nimmt, take, change to

noch, still

Note, notes

Notfall, necessity, *nur im Notfall zur,* only if necessary for

nur, only

offen, open, unstopped

ohne, without

Oktav(e), octave

Orchester, orchestra

Piston, cornet, *kleinem Piston,* small cornet in E♭

plötzlich, suddenly, *plözlichem,* sudden

Pralltriller, mordents

Pulte, desks, stands

recht, quite, very

Rhythmus, rhythm

roh(er), rough, crude

Rücksicht, regard

ruhevoll, peaceful

ruhig, calm

Saite, string

sanft, soft

Satz, movement

Schalltrichter, Schalltr., bells (of wind instruments)

Schlägeln, mallets

schlagen, beat, conduct

schleppen, drag

Schluss, end

schmetternd, blaring, resounding

schnell, fast, *schneller,* faster

Schwammschlägeln, sponge mallets

schwer, heavy

Schwung, energy

schwungvoll, energetically

sehr, very

selben, same

singend, singing

so . . . als, as . . . as

sofort, immediately

Sordinen, mutes

Spieler, players, *2. Spieler,* second group of 1st violins

spring. Bog., sautillé

stark, strongly, *stärker,* stronger, *stärker besetzt,* more players to a part

Steg, bridge

steigernd, intensifying

Steigerungen, increases

stetig, stets, steadily

Stimme, voice, group of 1st violins

Streicher, strings

streng, strictly

Strich, bowstroke, *Strich für Strich,* one bow per note, détaché

stürmen, rage, rush

summend, humming

Takt, beat, time

taktiren, tactiren, conduct, beat

Tellern, mit Tellern, clashed cymbals

Tempowechsel, change in tempo

Theilen, sections

tief(e), low, *tiefer,* lower

Ton, note, tone, sonority

Tönen, notes

Tonhöhe, register

Triangelschlägel, triangle beater

Triller, trill

Triolen, triplets

über, over, *über das ganze Orchester hinaus,* rising above the whole orchestra

Übergange, transition

übernimmt, takes, changes to

überraschend, surprisingly

übertönend, rising above, *alles übertönend,* louder than the rest of the orchestra

und, and

ungefähr, approximately

unmerklich, imperceptibly

Unterstützung, reinforcement, support

verändern, changing

verdoppelt, doubled

verhallend, becoming fainter

verklingend, dying away

Verlaufe, course

(sich) verlierend, dying away

Vermittlung, transition

verschwindend, disappearing

versehen, provided

versieht, plays

vibrirend, vibrating, with vibrato

viel, much, a lot of

Viertel, quarter-notes

Vokal, vowel

vollziehen, execute, *vollzieht sich,* to be executed

vom, by the

von, by

vorgetragen, played

vorhanden, (is) available

vorher, vorhin, before

Vorschläge, grace notes

vorwärts, pressing forward

wechseln, change

weich, soft, gently

Weise, tune, call

weiter, far, *weitester,* farthest

welche, which

wenig, little

wenn, if

werden, becoming

wie, as, as though

wieder, again

wild, unrestrained

womöglich, wo möglich, if possible

Worte, words

wuchtiger, more heavily, more vigorously

zart(e), gentle, gently, tenderly

Zeit, time

zögernd, hesitating

zu, to, in, at, *zu 2, 3, 4,* unisono

zuerst, at first

zufahrend, pressing, stringendo

zuletzt, just previously

zum, zur, to the

zurückhalten(d), meno mosso, *zurückhaltender,* more restrained

zurückkehren, return, *zurückkehrend,* returning

zwei, two

1., 2., 3., 4., 1st, 2nd, 3rd, 4th

2te, 3te, 4te, 2nd, 3rd, 4th

2(3,4) fach, in 2(3,4) parts

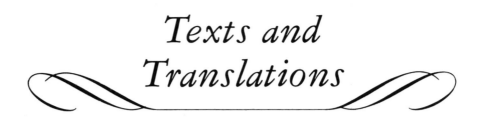

Texts and Translations

O Mensch! Gib Acht!
Was spricht die tiefe Mitternacht?
Ich schlief!
Aus tiefem Traum bin ich erwacht!
Die Welt ist tief!
und tiefer als der Tag gedacht!
O Mensch! Tief, tief ist ihr Weh!
Lust tiefer noch als Herzeleid!
Weh spricht: Vergeh!
Doch alle Lust will Ewigkeit!
will tiefe, tiefe Ewigkeit.

O man! Attend!
What says the deep midnight?
I slept!
From a deep dream have I awoken!
The world is deep!
and deeper than the day has imagined!
O man! Deep, deep is its suffering!
Joy deeper still than heart's sorrow!
Suffering speaks: Perish!
But all joy desires eternity!
desires deep, deep eternity.

From Nietzsche, *Also sprach Zarathustra*

ARMER KINDER BETTLERLIED

Es sungen drei Engel einen süssen Gesang;
mit Freuden es selig in dem Himmel klang,
sie jauchzten fröhlich auch dabei,
dass Petrus sei von Sünden frei,
er sei von Sünden frei.
Und als der Herr Jesus zu Tische sass,
mit seinen zwölf Jüngern das Abendmahl ass:
Da sprach der Herr Jesus: Was stehst du denn hier?
Wenn ich dich anseh', so weinest du mir!
Und sollt' ich nicht weinen, du gütiger Gott.
(Du sollst ja nicht weinen! Sollst ja nicht weinen!)
Ich hab' übertreten die zehn Gebot.
Ich gehe und weine ja bitterlich.
Ach komm und erbarme dich über mich!
Hast du denn übertreten die zehen Gebot,
so fall auf die Kniee und bete zu Gott!
Liebe nur Gott in alle Zeit!
So wirst du erlangen die himmlische Freud',
die himmlische Freud', die selige Stadt,
die himmlische Freude war Petro bereit't,
durch Jesum und allen zur Seligkeit.

POOR CHILDREN'S BEGGING SONG

Three angels were singing a sweet song;
with joy it resounded blissfully in heaven,
they rejoiced also
that Peter was free from sin,
he was free from sin.
And when the Lord Jesus sat at table,
with his twelve disciples ate the supper,
There spoke the Lord Jesus: What are you doing?
Whenever I look at you, I find you weeping!
And should I not weep, you gracious God.
(You should truly not weep! Should truly not weep!)
I have broken the Ten Commandments.
I go and weep most bitterly.
Ah, come and have mercy on me!
If you have broken the Ten Commandments,
then fall on your knees and pray to God!
Only love God forever!
Thus will you attain heavenly joy,
heavenly joy, the holy city,
heavenly joy was prepared for Peter
by Jesus and for all for their salvation.

From *Des Knaben Wunderhorn*

Das himmlische Leben

Wir geniessen die himmlische Freuden,
d'rum thun wir das Irdische meiden.
Kein weltlich' Getümmel hört man nicht im Himmel!
Lebt Alles in sanftester Ruh'!
Wir führen ein englisches Leben!
Sind dennoch ganz lustig daneben!
Wir tanzen und springen, wir hüpfen und singen!
Sanct Peter im Himmel sieht zu!
Johannes das Lämmlein auslasset,
der Metzger Herodes drauf passet!
Wir führen ein geduldig's, unschuldig's, geduldig's
ein liebliches Lämmlein zu Tod!
Sanct Lucas den Ochsen thät schlachten
ohn' einig's Bedenken und Achten,
der Wein kost kein Heller im himmlischen Keller,
die Englein, die backen das Brot.
Gut' Kräuter von allerhand Arten,
die wachsen im himmlischen Garten!
Gut' Spargel, Fisolen und was wir nur wollen!
Ganze Schüsseln voll sind uns bereit!
Gut' Äpfel, gut' Birn' und gut' Trauben!
die Gärtner, die Alles erlauben!
Willst Rehbock, willst Hasen auf offener Strassen
sie laufen herbei! Sollt ein Festtag etwa kommen
alle Fische gleich mit Freuden angeschwommen!
Dort läuft schon Sanct Peter mit Netz und mit Köder
zum himmlischen Weiher hinein.
Sanct Martha die Köchin muss sein!
Kein Musik ist ja nicht auf Erden,
die uns'rer verglichen kann werden.
Elf tausend Jungfrauen zu tanzen sich trauen!
Sanct Ursula selbst dazu lacht!
Kein Musik ist ja nicht auf Erden,
die uns'rer verglichen kann werden.
Cäcilia mit ihren Verwandten
sind treffliche Hofmusikanten!
Die englischen Stimmen ermuntern die Sinnen,
dass Alles für Freuden erwacht.

Heavenly Life

We enjoy the heavenly delights,
therefore do we shun the earthly.
No worldly tumult is heard in heaven!
All live in balmiest peace!
We lead an angelic life!
But we are quite merry at the same time!
We dance and skip, we frisk and sing!
Saint Peter in heaven looks on!
John lets out the little lamb,
The butcher Herod lies in wait for it!
We lead a patient, innocent, patient,
darling little lamb to its death!
St. Luke slaughters the ox
without any hesitation or concern,
the wine costs not a penny in the heavenly cellar,
the angels bake the bread.
Good vegetables of every kind
grow in the heavenly garden!
Good asparagus, beans and whatever we may desire!
Whole tureens-full are prepared for us!
Good apples, good pears and good grapes!
the gardeners make room for everything!
If you want deer or hare, they come running to you
along the open road! Should a fast day perchance arrive,
all the fish swim by at once gladly!
There runs Saint Peter already with net and with bait
into the heavenly fishpond.
Saint Martha must be the cook!
There is truly no music on earth
with which ours can be compared.
Eleven thousand maidens venture to dance!
Saint Ursula herself laughs to see it!
There is truly no music on earth
with which ours can be compared.
Cecilia and her relatives
are excellent court musicians!
The angel voices enliven the senses,
So that everyone awakes for joy.

From *Des Knaben Wunderhorn*

SYMPHONIES NOS. 3 and 4

IN FULL SCORE

SYMPHONY NO. 3

Instrumentation

4 Flutes [Fl.]
   (Fl. 3,4 = Piccolos [Picc.] 1,2)[1]
4 Oboes [Ob.]
   (Ob. 4 = English Horn [Engl. Horn, Englhr.])
3 Clarinets (B♭,A) [Clarinette, Cl. (B,A)][2]
   (Cl. 3 = Bass Clarinet (B♭) [Bassclarinette, Basscl.
     (B)])
2 E♭ Clarinets [Clarinette in Es, Cl. in Es][3]
   (E♭ Cl. 2 = Cl. 4)
4 Bassoons [Fagott, Fag.]
   (Bsn. 4 = Contrabassoon [Contrafagott, Ctrfag.])
8 Horns (F)
4 Trumpets (F,B♭) [Trompete, Trmp. (F,B)][4]
4 Trombones [Posaune, Pos.]
Contrabass Tuba [Contra-Bass Tuba, Tuba, Btb.]
2 Timpani [Pauke, Pk.], 3 drums each
2 Glockenspiels [Glockensp., Glcksp.], sounding an
   octave higher than notated
Tambourine [Tambr.]
Tam-tam
Triangle [Triangel, Trgl.]
Suspended Cymbal [Becken (freihängend), Beck.
   (frei)], to be reinforced by a second Cymbal
Side Drum [Kleine Trommel, Kl. Tr.]
Bass Drum [Grosse Trommel, Gr. Tr.]
Cymbal [Becken, Beck.], attached to the Bass Drum
   and struck with the drum by the same player
Switch [Ruthe], for striking the wood of the Bass
   Drum
2 Harps [Harfe]
Violins I, II [Violine,Viol.][5]
Violas
Cellos [Violoncell, Vcl.]
Basses [Contrabass, Cb.], some with low C-strings

Alto solo
Women's Choir [Frauenchor]

*In the distance [in der Ferne (Entfernung) auf-
gestellt]:*
   Flugelhorn (B♭) [Flügelh. (B)]
   Several Side Drums [kleine Trommeln]

In a high gallery [in der Höhe postiert]:
   4 (if possible, 5 or 6) tuned Bells [abgestimmte
     Glocken, Glocken]
   Boys' Choir [Knabenchor]

The symphony is divided into two parts. Part 1
consists of movement I, Part 2 of movements II, III,
IV, V, and VI. After Part 1 a long pause.

Note: All trills are to be performed without final turns
[Nachschläge], even where this is not explicitly stated.

---

[1]At two points (1st and 5th movements), 4 piccolos are used
   (in place of 4 flutes).
[2]Cl. 1 doubled if possible.
[3]Reinforced if possible in 5th movement.
[4]2 more high trumpets to be used for reinforcing if possible. E♭
   Cornet to be substituted for Tpt. 1 at one point in 1st
   movement if possible.
[5]Very large complements of all strings.

SYMPHONIE No.3.
I. Abtheilung.
No.1.

Kräftig. Entschieden.

1.2. Flöte.	
3.4. Flöte.(1.2.Piccolo.)	
1.2.3. Oboe.	
4. Oboe. (engl. Horn.)	
1.2. Clarinette in B.	
3.Clarinette in B. (Bassel.)	
1.2. Clarinette in Es.	
1.2.3. Fagott.	ff
4. Fagott. (Contrafag.)	ff
1.2.3.4.5.6.7.8.Horn in F.	zu 8 ff
1.2.3.4. Trompete in F.	
1.2.3.4. Posaune.	1.2. f
Contra – Basstuba.	ff
Glockenspiel. Kl.Trommel.	kl.Tr. ff
Triangel. Tambourin.	
Becken (freihängend.) Tamtam.	
Becken. an der gr. Trommel befestigt und vom selben Musiker geschlagen, der die Trommel versieht.	gr.Tr. 1.
Gr. Trommel.	
1.2. Pauke.	1.in A,B,E hoch. 2.in D tief,B,F hoch. ff
1.2. Harfe.	
1.Violine.	G-Saite ff
2.Violine.	G-Saite ff
Viola.	ff
Violoncell.	ff
Contrabass.	ff

Kräftig. Entschieden.

Anmerkung für den Dirigenten: Das Anfangstempo ist im Ganzen und Grossen für das ganze Stück durchaus festzuhalten und trotz der jeweiligen Taktwechsel oder Modificationen strengste Continuität desselben durchzuführen.

Note for the conductor: The opening tempo is, for the most part, to be retained throughout the whole movement, and the strictest continuity of tempo is to be maintained in spite of momentary changes in beat or modifications.

*) Diese Triolen schnell, ungefähr mit den Vorschlägen der grossen Trommel zusammen.

*)These triplets *fast*, approximately simultaneously with those on the bass drum.

* Diese Triole immer, unter allen Umständen, **schnell** auszuführen!

*These triplets always, under all conditions, to be performed *fast!*

16 Etwas drängend.
zu 2
Vorwärts.
1. 2. Cl. in B.
trem.
Bassel. in B.
trem.
zu 3
1. 2. 3. Fag.
trem.
Ctrfag.
16 Etwas drängend.
zu 2
Vorwärts.
1. 3. Horn in F.
zu 2
2. 5. Horn in F.
zu 2
4. 7. Horn in F.
zu 2
6. 8.
1.
Triolen nicht schleppend.
Wild.
acc.
cresc.
Pos.
zu 2
2. 3. Pos.
Wild.
4.
Btb.
16 Etwas drängend.
Vorwärts.
Gr. Tr.
Des nach D.
1. Pk. 2.
molto cresc.
geth.
Viola.
cresc.
Vcl.
geth.
cresc.
Cb.

* **das A der I. Tr. ist kein Druckfehler.**

*The A in the 1st Trumpet is *not* a typographical error.

*) **Anmerkung für den Dirigenten**: Diese Stelle muss von den Streichern mit höchster Kraftentfaltung gespielt werden, so dass die Saiten durch die heftige Vibration beinahe in Berührung mit dem Griffbrett gerathen. Der Wiener hat dafür den Ausdruck: „schöppern." Ein gleiches gilt von den Hörnern.

*)*Note for the conductor:* This passage must be played by the strings with the greatest power, so that the individual strings, as a result of the violent vibration, almost come in contact with the fingerboard. The Viennese call this "schöppern." A similar effect applies to the horns.

Immer noch drängend.

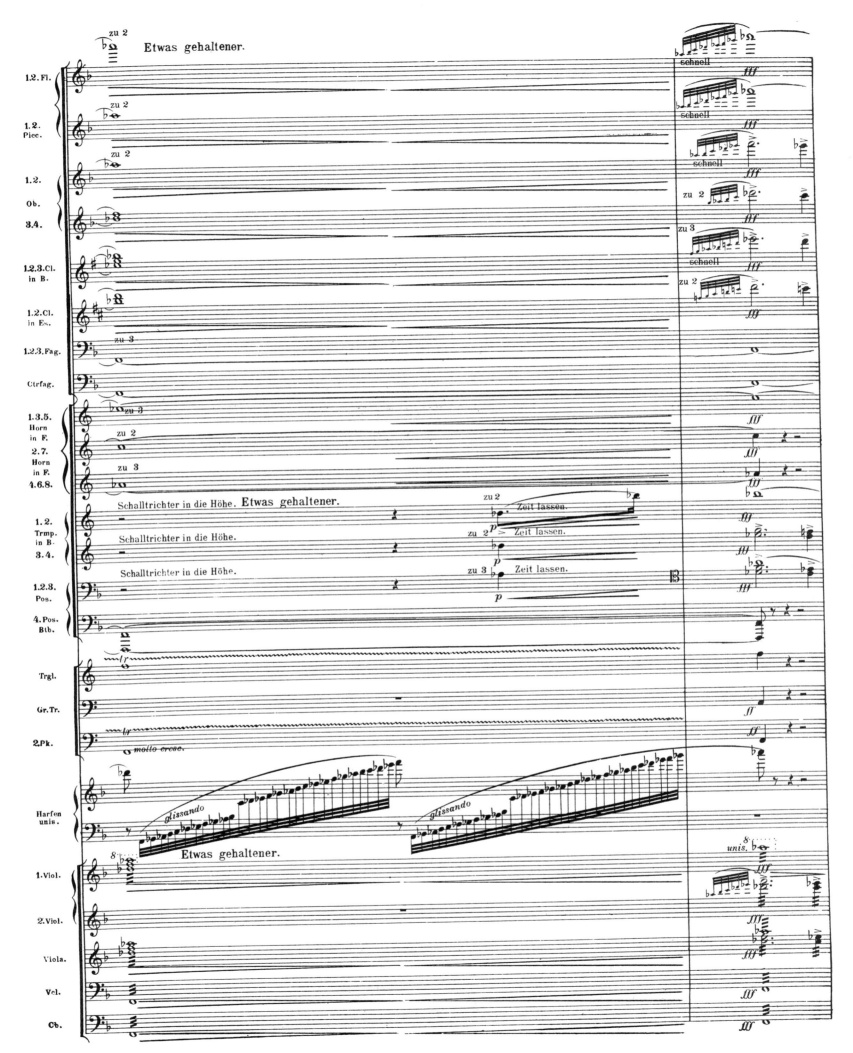

Zweite Abtheilung.
№ 2.

(Von ✳ bis ✳ kann das engl. Horn zuhilfe genommen werden, wenn der Oboist die Stelle nicht zart genug hervorbringen kann.)

(From * to * the English horn can be substituted if the oboist cannot perform the passage softly enough.)

№ 3.

Anmerkung für den Dirigenten: ✱ **ohne** Rücksicht auf das Tempo.

Note for the conductor: *Fanfare—without regard for the tempo.

+) *Anmerkung für den Dirigenten.* Kein Irrthum! Mit dem Rücken des Bogens gestrichen!

Note for the conductor: Not an error! Bowed with the back of the bow!

№ 4.

Worte von Nietzsche.

179

N.B. Zu dieser Stelle sind durchaus nur Bässe mit der tiefen Contra C-Saite zu benützen.

N.B. *Throughout* this passage *only basses* with *low C-strings* are to be used.

Nº 5.

Worte aus des „Knaben Wunderhorn".

190

*) Der Ton ist dem Klang einer Glocke nachzuahmen, der Vocal kurz anzuschlagen und der Ton durch den Consonanten M summend auszuhalten.

*)The note should imitate the sound of a bell, the vowel attacked briefly and the note sustained by humming on the consonant *m*.

NB. Diese 4 Takte werden geschlagen, wenn noch eine 5. Glocke in B vorhanden ist.

N.B. These four measures are to be played if a fifth bell in B♭ is available.

№ 6.

*) Anmerkung für den Dirigenten: Hier ist das Tempo im Verlaufe der unmerklichen Steigerung ungefähr noch einmal so schnell geworden wie zu Anfang. (aber immer noch in Vierteln zu taktiren)

*Note for the conductor: Here the tempo, in the course of the almost imperceptible accelerando, again becomes approximately as fast as at the beginning (but is always to be conducted in quarter-notes).

*) Anmerkung für den Dirigenten: Um die grösste Intensität des Tones zu erzielen, wechseln die Geiger möglichst oft, aber unmerklich, den Bogen.

*)Note for the conductor: In order to attain the greatest intensity of tone, the violins should change bows as often as possible, but inaudibly.

220

SYMPHONY NO. 4

Instrumentation

4 Flutes [Flöte, Fl.]
  (Fl. 3,4 = Piccolo [Picc.] 1,2)
3 Oboes [Ob.]
  (Ob. 3 = English Horn [Englisch Horn, Englh.])
3 Clarinets (A,B♭,C) [Clarinette, Cl.]
  (Cl. 2 = E♭ Clarinet [Cl. in Es] ; Cl. 3 = Bass Clarinet
  (A,B♭) [Bassclarinet, Bcl. (A,B)])
3 Bassoons [Fagott, Fag.]
  (Bsn. 3 = Contrabassoon [Contrafagott, Ctrfag.])
4 Horns (F)
3 Trumpets (F,B♭) [Trompete,Trp. (F,B)]
Timpani [Pauke, Pk.]
Sleighbells [Schelle, Sch.]
Cymbals [Becken, Bck.]
Glockenspiel [Glspl.]
Triangle [Triangel, Trgl.]
Tam-tam
Bass Drum [Grosse Trommel, Gr. Tr.]
Harp [Harfe, Hfe.]
Violins I, II [Violine, Vl.]
Violas [Vla.]
Cellos [Violoncell, Vlc.]
Basses [Contrabass, Cb.]

Soprano [Singstimme, Singst.]

SYMPHONIE № 4.

I.

+ Zeichen für einzelne gestopfte Töne.

+ Symbol for individual stopped tones.

NB. Klingt eine Octave tiefer.

II.

N.B. Der I. Sologeiger hat sich mit 2 Instrumenten zu versehen, von denen das eine um einen Ganzton höher, das andere normal gestimmt ist.

N.B. The 1st solo violin must be provided with two instruments, one tuned a whole-tone higher, the other tuned normally.

NB. Der 2. Spieler am ersten Pult hat mit den ANDERN zu spielen.
N.B. The 2nd player at the first desk must play with the OTHER violins.

III.

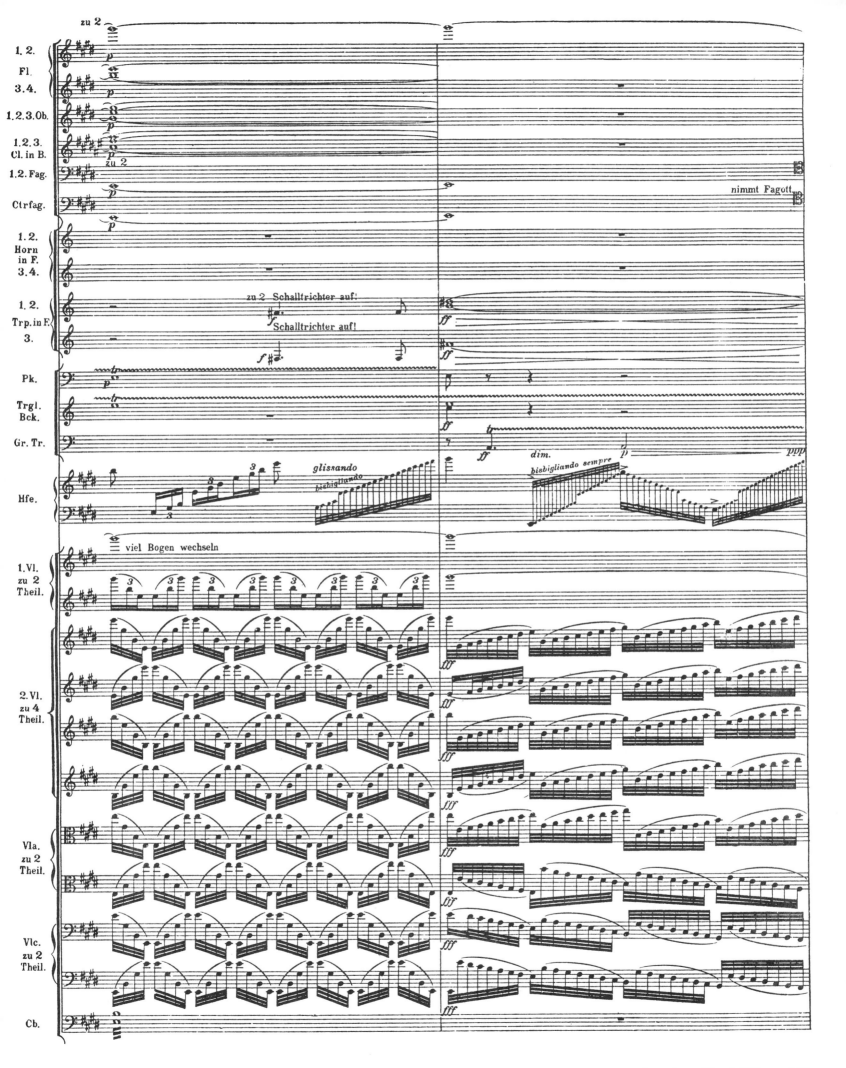

Anmerkung für den Dirigenten: Es ist von höchster Wichtigkeit, dass die Sängerin äusserst discret begleitet wird.

Note for the conductor: It is of the greatest importance that the singer be *extremely* discreetly accompanied.

IV.

Gedicht aus „Des Knaben Wunderhorn."

NB. Singstimme mit kindlich heiterem Ausdruck; durchaus ohne Parodie!

N.B. To be sung with childlike and serene expression; absolutely without parody!

*) Hier muss dieses Tempo bewegter genommen werden, als an den correspondierenden Stellen im ersten Satze.
*) Here this tempo must be taken faster than at the corresponding passages in the first movement.

Dover Orchestral Scores

THE SIX BRANDENBURG CONCERTOS AND THE FOUR ORCHESTRAL SUITES IN FULL SCORE, Johann Sebastian Bach. Complete standard Bach-Gesellschaft editions in large, clear format. Study score. 273pp. 9 × 12.   23376-6 Pa. **$10.95**

COMPLETE CONCERTI FOR SOLO KEYBOARD AND ORCHESTRA IN FULL SCORE, Johann Sebastian Bach. Bach's seven complete concerti for solo keyboard and orchestra in full score from the authoritative Bach-Gesellschaft edition. 206pp. 9 × 12.
24929-8 Pa. **$9.95**

THE THREE VIOLIN CONCERTI IN FULL SCORE, Johann Sebastian Bach. Concerto in A Minor, BWV 1041; Concerto in E Major, BWV 1042; and Concerto for Two Violins in D Minor, BWV 1043. Bach-Gesellschaft edition. 64pp. 9⅜ × 12¼.   25124-1 Pa. **$5.95**

GREAT ORGAN CONCERTI, OPP. 4 & 7, IN FULL SCORE, George Frideric Handel. 12 organ concerti composed by great Baroque master are reproduced in full score from the *Deutsche Handelgesellschaft* edition. 138pp. 9⅜ × 12¼.   24462-8 Pa. **$7.95**

COMPLETE CONCERTI GROSSI IN FULL SCORE, George Frideric Handel. Monumental Opus 6 Concerti Grossi, Opus 3 and "Alexander's Feast" Concerti Grossi—19 in all—reproduced from most authoritative edition. 258pp. 9⅜ × 12¼.   24187-4 Pa. **$11.95**

COMPLETE CONCERTI GROSSI IN FULL SCORE, Arcangelo Corelli. All 12 concerti in the famous late nineteenth-century edition prepared by violinist Joseph Joachim and musicologist Friedrich Chrysander. 240pp. 8⅜ × 11¼.   25606-5 Pa. **$11.95**

WATER MUSIC AND MUSIC FOR THE ROYAL FIREWORKS IN FULL SCORE, George Frideric Handel. Full scores of two of the most popular Baroque orchestral works performed today—reprinted from definitive Deutsche Handelgesellschaft edition. Total of 96pp. 8¼ × 11.   25070-9 Pa. **$5.95**

LATER SYMPHONIES, Wolfgang A. Mozart. Full orchestral scores to last symphonies (Nos. 35–41) reproduced from definitive Breitkopf & Härtel Complete Works edition. Study score. 285pp. 9 × 12.
23052-X Pa. **$11.95**

17 DIVERTIMENTI FOR VARIOUS INSTRUMENTS, Wolfgang A. Mozart. Sparkling pieces of great vitality and brilliance from 1771–1779; consecutively numbered from 1 to 17. Reproduced from definitive Breitkopf & Härtel Complete Works edition. Study score. 241pp. 9⅜ × 12¼.   23862-8 Pa. **$11.95**

PIANO CONCERTOS NOS. 11–16 IN FULL SCORE, Wolfgang Amadeus Mozart. Authoritative Breitkopf & Härtel edition of six staples of the concerto repertoire, including Mozart's cadenzas for Nos. 12–16. 256pp. 9⅜ × 12¼.   25468-2 Pa. **$11.95**

PIANO CONCERTOS NOS. 17–22, Wolfgang Amadeus Mozart. Six complete piano concertos in full score, with Mozart's own cadenzas for Nos. 17–19. Breitkopf & Härtel edition. Study score. 370pp. 9⅜ × 12¼.   23599-8 Pa. **$14.95**

PIANO CONCERTOS NOS. 23–27, Wolfgang Amadeus Mozart. Mozart's last five piano concertos in full score, plus cadenzas for Nos. 23 and 27, and the Concert Rondo in D Major, K.382. Breitkopf & Härtel edition. Study score. 310pp. 9⅜ × 12¼.   23600-5 Pa. **$11.95**

CONCERTI FOR WIND INSTRUMENTS IN FULL SCORE, Wolfgang Amadeus Mozart. Exceptional volume contains ten pieces for orchestra and wind instruments and includes some of Mozart's finest, most popular music. 272pp. 9⅜ × 12¼.   25228-0 Pa. **$12.95**

THE VIOLIN CONCERTI AND THE SINFONIA CONCERTANTE, K.364, IN FULL SCORE, Wolfgang Amadeus Mozart. All five violin concerti and famed double concerto reproduced from authoritative Breitkopf & Härtel Complete Works Edition. 208pp. 9⅜ × 12½.   25169-1 Pa. **$10.95**

SYMPHONIES 88–92 IN FULL SCORE: The Haydn Society Edition, Joseph Haydn. Full score of symphonies Nos. 88 through 92. Large, readable noteheads, ample margins for fingerings, etc., and extensive Editor's Commentary. 304pp. 9 × 12. (Available in U.S. only)
24445-8 Pa. **$13.95**

COMPLETE LONDON SYMPHONIES IN FULL SCORE, Series I and Series II, Joseph Haydn. Reproduced from the Eulenburg editions are Symphonies Nos. 93–98 (Series I) and Nos. 99–104 (Series II). 800pp. 8⅜ × 11¼. (Available in U.S. only)   Series I 24982-4 Pa. **$14.95**
Series II 24983-2 Pa. **$15.95**

FOUR SYMPHONIES IN FULL SCORE, Franz Schubert. Schubert's four most popular symphonies: No. 4 in C Minor ("Tragic"); No. 5 in B-flat Major; No. 8 in B Minor ("Unfinished"); and No. 9 in C Major ("Great"). Breitkopf & Härtel edition. Study score. 261pp. 9⅜ × 12¼.   23681-1 Pa. **$11.95**

GREAT OVERTURES IN FULL SCORE, Carl Maria von Weber. Overtures to *Oberon, Der Freischutz, Euryanthe* and *Preciosa* reprinted from authoritative Breitkopf & Härtel editions. 112pp. 9 × 12.
25225-6 Pa. **$6.95**

SYMPHONIES NOS. 1, 2, 3, AND 4 IN FULL SCORE, Ludwig van Beethoven. Republication of H. Litolff edition. 272pp. 9 × 12.
26033-X Pa. **$10.95**

SYMPHONIES NOS. 5, 6 AND 7 IN FULL SCORE, Ludwig van Beethoven. Republication of the H. Litolff edition. 272pp. 9 × 12.
26034-8 Pa. **$10.95**

SYMPHONIES NOS. 8 AND 9 IN FULL SCORE, Ludwig van Beethoven. Republication of the H. Litolff edition. 256pp. 9 × 12.
26035-6 Pa. **$10.95**

SIX GREAT OVERTURES IN FULL SCORE, Ludwig van Beethoven. Six staples of the orchestral repertoire from authoritative Breitkopf & Härtel edition. *Leonore Overtures,* Nos. 1–3; Overtures to *Coriolanus, Egmont, Fidelio.* 288pp. 9 × 12.   24789-9 Pa. **$12.95**

COMPLETE PIANO CONCERTOS IN FULL SCORE, Ludwig van Beethoven. Complete scores of five great Beethoven piano concertos, with all cadenzas as he wrote them, reproduced from authoritative Breitkopf & Härtel edition. New table of contents. 384pp. 9⅜ × 12¼.   24563-2 Pa. **$14.95**

GREAT ROMANTIC VIOLIN CONCERTI IN FULL SCORE, Ludwig van Beethoven, Felix Mendelssohn and Peter Ilyitch Tchaikovsky. The Beethoven Op. 61, Mendelssohn, Op. 64 and Tchaikovsky, Op. 35 concertos reprinted from the Breitkopf & Härtel editions. 224pp. 9 × 12.   24989-1 Pa. **$10.95**

MAJOR ORCHESTRAL WORKS IN FULL SCORE, Felix Mendelssohn. Generally considered to be Mendelssohn's finest orchestral works, here in one volume are: the complete *Midsummer Night's Dream; Hebrides Overture; Calm Sea and Prosperous Voyage Overture;* Symphony No. 3 in A ("Scottish"); and Symphony No. 4 in A ("Italian"). Breitkopf & Härtel edition. Study score. 406pp. 9 × 12.   23184-4 Pa. **$15.95**

COMPLETE SYMPHONIES, Johannes Brahms. Full orchestral scores. No. 1 in C Minor, Op. 68; No. 2 in D Major, Op. 73; No. 3 in F Major, Op. 90; and No. 4 in E Minor, Op. 98. Reproduced from definitive Vienna Gesellschaft der Musikfreunde edition. Study score. 344pp. 9 × 12.   23053-8 Pa. **$13.95**